THEMATIC UNIT
Grandparents

Written by Deborah Plona Cerbus, M.A.
and
Cheryl Feichtenbiner Rice, M.A

Teacher Created Materials, Inc.
P.O. Box 1040
Huntington Beach, CA 92647
©1997 Teacher Created Materials, Inc.
Made in U.S.A.

ISBN 1-57690-112-2

Illustrator:
Ken Tunell
Editor:
Jeri Wilcox
Cover Artist:
Sue Fullam

The classroom teacher may reproduce copies of materials in this book for classroom use only. The reproduction of any part for an entire school or school system is strictly prohibited. No part of this publication may be transmitted, stored, or recorded in any form without written permission from the publisher.

Table of Contents

Introduction

Grandparents contains an exciting primary thematic unit. Its 80 pages are filled with a variety of ideas and activities designed for use with primary children. At its core are two quality children's literature selections, *Tanya's Reunion* (sequel to *The Patchwork Quilt*) and *Grandfather's Lovesong*. For these books, activities are included which set the stage for reading, encourage the enjoyment of the book, and extend the concepts which were introduced in the books. In addition, the theme is integrated into the curriculum through activities in language arts (including daily writing suggestions), math, science (learning about precipitation and farm animals), social studies, art, music, and life skills (cooking and games). Hands-on and minds-on learning and cooperative group activities are woven throughout the unit.

The culminating activity provides directions for a Grandparents Gala. This activity is designed to showcase the students' learning and help the children integrate what they have learned into a special day of fun for them to share with their grandparents or other special friends.

Although this book is addressed to children and their grandparents, some children may not have the opportunity to enjoy the grandparent experience. Some grandparents may live far away, some may no longer be living, and others may not be actively involved in the lives of their grandchildren. For these children, the ideas in books about grandparents and their grandchildren spending time together and sharing experiences may be particularly important. It will be necessary for the teacher to be sensitive to the feelings of these children in planning activities for the classroom. In instances where children are asked to do an activity with a grandparent, another family member, a family friend, or adult school friend may be involved in the activity instead of a grandparent.

This *Grandparents* thematic unit includes the following features:

- ❏ **literature selections**—summaries of two children's books with related lessons (complete with reproducible pages) that integrate activities throughout the curriculum

- ❏ **planning guides**—suggestions for sequencing lessons each day of the unit

- ❏ **writing ideas**—daily suggestions as well as writing activities across the curriculum, including Big Books

- ❏ **curriculum connections**—in language arts, math, science, social studies, art, music, and life skills such as cooking and games

- ❏ **bulletin board ideas**—suggestions and plans for student-created bulletin boards

- ❏ **homework suggestions**—extending the unit to the students' homes

- ❏ **group projects**—to encourage cooperative learning

- ❏ **a culminating activity**—to require students to synthesize their learning and engage in activities that will be shared with others

- ❏ **a bibliography**—suggestions of additional fiction and nonfiction materials to correlate with the theme

> **To keep this valuable resource intact so that it can be used year after year, you may wish to punch holes in the pages and store them in a three-ring binder.**

Introduction (cont.)

Why Balance Basic Skills and Whole Language?

The strength of a whole language approach is that it involves children in using all modes of communication—reading, writing, listening, illustrating, and interacting. Communication skills are interconnected and integrated into lessons that emphasize the whole of language. Balancing this approach is our knowledge that every whole is composed of parts, and directed study of those parts can help a student to master the whole. Experience and research tell us that regular attention to phonics, other word attack skills, spelling, etc., develops reading mastery, thereby completing the unity of the whole language experience. The child is thus led to read, write, spell, speak, and listen confidently in response to a literature experience introduced by the teacher. In these ways, language skills grow rapidly, stimulated by direct practice, involvement, and interest in the topic at hand.

Why Thematic Planning?

One very useful tool for implementing an integrated whole language program is thematic planning. By choosing a theme with correlating literature selections for a unit of study, a teacher can plan activities throughout the day that lead to a cohesive in-depth study of the topic. Students will be practicing and applying their skills in meaningful context, so that they will tend to learn and retain more from the activities.

Why Cooperative Learning?

In addition to academic skills and content, students need to learn social skills. This area of development may no longer be taken for granted. Students must learn to work cooperatively in groups in order to function well in today's society. Group activities should be a regular part of school life, and teachers should consciously include social objectives as well as academic objectives in their planning.

Why Big Books?

An excellent, cooperative, whole language activity is the production of Big Books. Groups of students or the whole class can apply their language skills, content knowledge, and creativity to produce a Big Book that can become a part of the classroom to be read and reread. These books make excellent culminating projects for sharing beyond the classroom with parents, librarians, and other classes. Big Books can be produced in many ways. This thematic resource book includes directions for creating Big Books that you may choose to use in your classroom.

Why Journals?

Each day your students should have the opportunity to write in journals. They may respond to a book, write about a personal experience, or answer a general "question of the day" posed by the teacher. The cumulative journal provides an excellent means of documenting writing progress and a means of assessment.

Tanya's Reunion

by Valerie Flournoy

Summary

In this sequel to *The Patchwork Quilt*, Tanya and her family are gathering for a family reunion. Tanya travels to the farm in Virginia with her grandmother and is disappointed at first by what she sees. But as Tanya explores the farm with her grandmother, she discovers special memories and the rich history of her family. This book is a loving tribute to the special bond that exists between a grandparent and grandchild and demonstrates how much can be gained by reflecting on our heritage.

The outline below is a suggested five-day plan for using the various activities that are presented in this unit. These ideas can be adapted as needed to fit your own classroom situation.

Sample Plan

Day 1

- Read *Tanya's Reunion* using some of the Enjoying the Book activities. (page 7)
- Introduce the family card writing center. (page 6)
- Begin Daily Writing Topics. (page 9)
- Start to prepare for the Grandparents' Gala. (page 74)

Day 2

- Read another book about grandparents. (You may want to choose one from the bibliography on page 79)
- Compare the book to *Tanya's Reunion* using the chart on page 10.
- Learn about the presidents who came from Virginia by starting the Extending the Book activities on page 8.
- Begin the Apple a Day thinking skills. (pages 12 and 13)
- Learn the song about Grandma's farm. (page 69)
- Continue the Daily Writing Topics. (page 9)

Day 3

- Teach the class an old-fashioned game. (page 73)
- Create a card or postcard to send to grandma or grandpa. (pages 64 and 65)
- Locate a farm in your area and schedule a class trip. Other ideas for a trip might be visiting a one-room school, a log cabin, or a museum.
- Write a class Big Book following your field trip. Enlarge the book cover, Our Day on the Farm. (page 11)

- Continue Daily Writing Topics. (page 9)
- Continue Apple a Day thinking skills. (pages 12 and 13)

Day 4

- Prepare the Grandparent Puzzle. (page 66)
- Practice money skills with Bus Fare Math. (pages 14–16)
- Learn more of the songs in the music section to perform at the gala. (pages 68–70)
- Continue the An Apple a Day thinking skills. (pages 12 and 13)
- Brainstorm a list of farm animals. Do the farm research project. (pages 56–58)
- Continue the Daily Writing Topics. (page 9)

Day 5

- Learn about the author with Meet Valerie Flournoy. (page 41)
- Practice math skills with Farm Story Problems. (pages 17–19)
- Finish the Extending the Book activities. (page 8)
- Complete the An Apple a Day thinking skills (pages 12 and 13) and display the students' work on a bulletin board.
- Continue the Daily Writing Topics. (page 9)
- Finish preparations for the Grandparents' Gala. (page 74)
- Have the class make and send invitations for this special event.

Overview of Activities

Setting the Stage

1. Prepare your reading corner for this unit by putting out a display of books about grandparents. See the bibliography on page 79 for some selections. Add a cozy rocking chair for grandparents to sit in when they visit. Put a lace or crocheted tablecloth on your book table to create an old fashioned look for the book display. Bring in some antiques such as books, quilts, and kitchen tools for the class to enjoy. Since antique items may be unfamiliar to the children, try the following guessing game activity. Put out a different antique each day and write three clues on a chalkboard slate as to what it was used for in the past. Have the children write their guesses on paper and put the slips in an "old fashioned" tin container such as the ones that cookies are sold in around the holidays. At the end of the day, reveal the name of the antique and for what it was used.

2. Tanya and her grandmother enjoy baking day in the story. If you have a dramatic play center in your classroom, set up a baking center. Stock it with different types of equipment such as cupcake tins, pie plates, and cookie sheets. Add spoons and cups in a variety of sizes for some practice in measuring skills. Print some simple "no bake" recipes in the center for the children to make, such as mini peanut butter and jelly sandwiches. (For recipes, see page 71)

3. Bring in your own family album to share with the class. Show pictures of your grandparents and talk about some of your favorite family memories and stories. Encourage the children to tell the class about their grandparents. Be sure to be sensitive to the feelings of children who don't have any grandparents. These children can share memories about other family members.

4. Create a family card writing center. Provide a variety of paper, markers, crayons, and colored pencils for making cards for grandparents and other family members. Include other materials such as stickers, wrapping paper, and used greeting cards. If you have access to a computer, students may also make cards using one of the commercially made graphics programs available for computers.

5. Duplicate the letter on page 75 and send it home. Start getting ready for the Grandparents' Gala on page 74.

6. Prepare a bulletin board for the Grandparents' Gallery. (See activity on page 21)

7. Make a word web about grandparents. A word web is a good way to organize ideas about a topic. Start by writing the word "grandparents" in a circle either on the chalkboard or in the center of a piece of chart paper. Ask the class to think of words that relate to grandparents and arrange the words to form a "web" of connected circles.

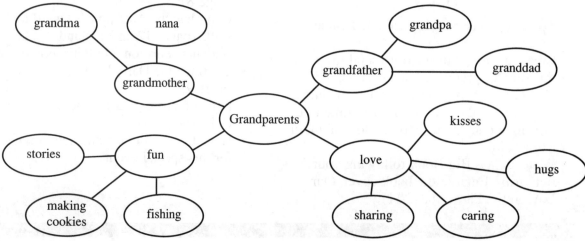

Overview of Activities *(cont.)*

Enjoying the Book

1. Bring in several quilts and lay them on the floor. Invite the class to sit on the quilts as they listen to the story. Show the cover of the book and have the students read the title. Discuss what a reunion is. Ask if anyone has ever been to a family reunion.

2. Introduce and discuss some of the vocabulary in the story which may be unfamiliar to your students. Some suggested words are homestead, parlor, pasture, till, orchard, harvest, history, holler, and blacksmith. Be sure to read the words in a sentence so that students can practice using context clues to figure out the meaning of the new words. Older students may want to use a dictionary for the new vocabulary.

3. Define "setting" as being where a story takes place. Since the setting of this story is primarily on a farm, activate students' prior knowledge by having the students brainstorm what they know about a farm. This could be done in the form of a K-W-L activity, where students tell what they Know, what they Want to know, and what they have Learned. The information can be written on a large chart as the topic is discussed.

4. Read *Tanya's Reunion* to the class. Pause every two or three pages to talk about the story. Take time to look at and discuss the beautiful illustrations by Jerry Pinkney, who is an award winning artist and illustrator. Ask the class how Tanya's feelings change about the farm as the story progresses.

5. Talk about different family members who may come to a reunion. Make a list of family words (mother, father, grandmother, grandfathers, aunt, uncle, etc.) for later use in the family card writing center. You may also want to include a list of words and phrases commonly found on cards such as Thank You and Happy Birthday.

Overview of Activities *(cont.)*

Extending the Book

1. Grandma's farm was located in Virginia. Find Virginia on a map of the United States (page 77) and compare it with the state in which you live. Some comparisons could include differences in size, climate, terrain, crops, and industry.

2. Tanya learns from Grandma that four of the first five presidents of the United States were born in Virginia. Do some research to find out the names of these presidents and the years that they served. One excellent resource for information on the presidents is *The Buck Stops Here* by Alice Provensen. For another social studies activity relating to presidents see Who Was President When My Grandparents and Parents Were My Age? (page 60)

3. Read *The Patchwork Quilt*, the first book about Tanya and her grandmother. Compare the family stories by Valerie Flournoy with another classic story, *The Relatives Came* by Cynthia Rylant. As you discuss how the stories are the same or different, talk about important story elements such as characters, setting, problems, how problems are solved, and the mood of the story. Complete the Book Comparison Chart found on page 10 for an in depth study of these two stories. Read one or two books about grandparents each day during this unit.

4. Take a field trip to a local farm to learn more about life in the country. Following the trip, write a class book with each child contributing a page about what has been learned and an accompanying illustration. A cover for the book, Our Day on the Farm, is provided on page 11.

5. For science, have the children do individual research about a farm animal that interests them using the Farm Animal Research Booklet found on pages 56 through 58.

6. Expand your students' understanding of the story by asking questions which involve higher level thinking skills. Use the An Apple a Day . . . questions provided on page 12. These may be used as writing center activities or as daily class assignments.

7. Tanya and her grandmother travel on the bus to the farm. Conduct a survey to determine how students travel to their grandparents' house and complete the Family Travels bar graph on page 46.

8. Make a link to your math curriculum by completing the Bus Fare Math activity on pages 14–16. This can be placed at the math center or taught as a whole class activity.

9. Practice story problem skills by using the Farm Story Problems found on pages 17-19. Students may color the farm scene and then use it to solve the story problems found on the worksheet. The farm scene could also be duplicated on construction paper or tagboard and laminated for use at the math center. Additional story problems to solve could be supplied by the teacher or made up by older children. Their problems could be written on a small dry erase board and left in the center for the next group of students to solve. A problem of the day could also be written on the chalkboard for the class to solve as they enter the classroom in the morning.

10. Introduce the children to some classic games such as dominoes, checkers, and hopscotch. Try some of the games found in *Games of Long Ago* by Bobbie Kalman. If you have indoor recess toys, add games such as jacks and pick up sticks. Some of these games can be taught to the class and played during the Grandparents' Gala, the culminating activity for this unit. See page 74.

        8

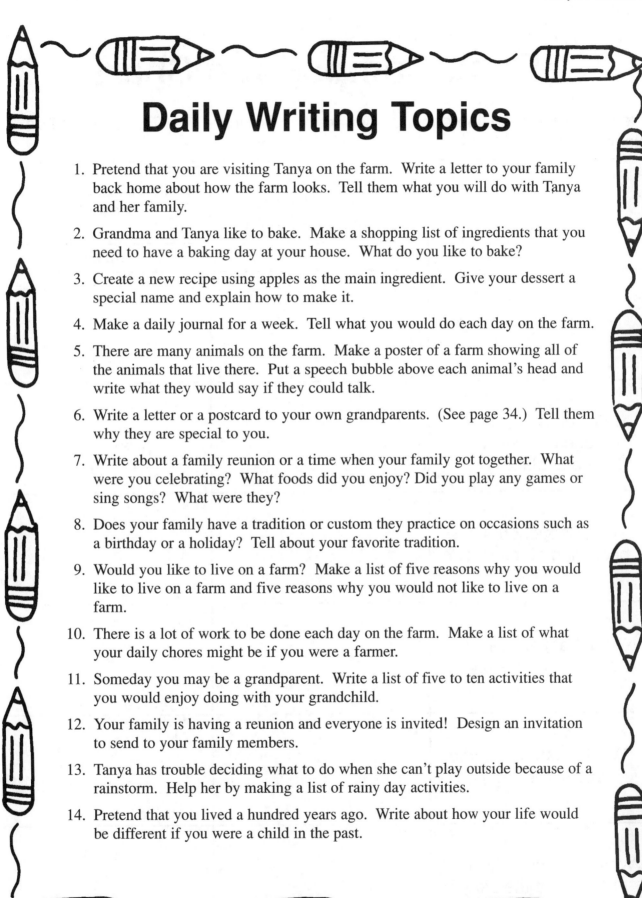

Daily Writing Topics

1. Pretend that you are visiting Tanya on the farm. Write a letter to your family back home about how the farm looks. Tell them what you will do with Tanya and her family.

2. Grandma and Tanya like to bake. Make a shopping list of ingredients that you need to have a baking day at your house. What do you like to bake?

3. Create a new recipe using apples as the main ingredient. Give your dessert a special name and explain how to make it.

4. Make a daily journal for a week. Tell what you would do each day on the farm.

5. There are many animals on the farm. Make a poster of a farm showing all of the animals that live there. Put a speech bubble above each animal's head and write what they would say if they could talk.

6. Write a letter or a postcard to your own grandparents. (See page 34.) Tell them why they are special to you.

7. Write about a family reunion or a time when your family got together. What were you celebrating? What foods did you enjoy? Did you play any games or sing songs? What were they?

8. Does your family have a tradition or custom they practice on occasions such as a birthday or a holiday? Tell about your favorite tradition.

9. Would you like to live on a farm? Make a list of five reasons why you would like to live on a farm and five reasons why you would not like to live on a farm.

10. There is a lot of work to be done each day on the farm. Make a list of what your daily chores might be if you were a farmer.

11. Someday you may be a grandparent. Write a list of five to ten activities that you would enjoy doing with your grandchild.

12. Your family is having a reunion and everyone is invited! Design an invitation to send to your family members.

13. Tanya has trouble deciding what to do when she can't play outside because of a rainstorm. Help her by making a list of rainy day activities.

14. Pretend that you lived a hundred years ago. Write about how your life would be different if you were a child in the past.

Book Comparison Chart

Read another selection about grandparents. Compare it to *Tanya's Reunion* using the chart.

	Tanya's Reunion by Valerie Flournoy	Book Title _____ Author
Names of Characters		
Setting (When and where does the story take place?)		
What happened at the beginning of the story?		
What happened in the middle of the story?		
What happened at the end of the story?		
What was the main idea or theme of the story?		

10

Our Day on the Farm

Written and Illustrated by

An Apple a Day...

To Develop Thinking Skills

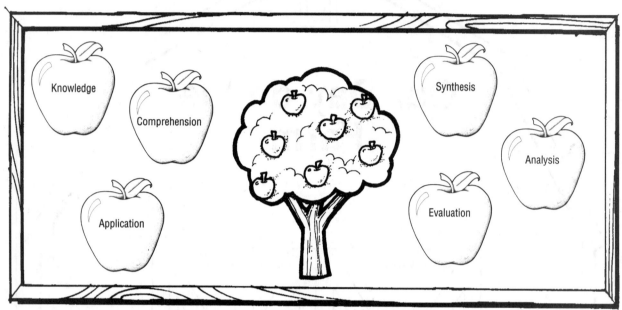

Directions: Enlarge and duplicate the apple shapes on red, yellow, or green construction paper or tagboard and laminate for durability. The questions may be used "one a day" as a follow up to the story. Have students write their responses on blank apple shapes which could be made by tracing and cutting the pattern provided or by using commercially made apple-shape note pads. Student answers can be saved and assembled as a class book or put on a bulletin board on a tree shape. To construct the tree, twist brown butcher paper for the trunk and branches. Have students trace around their hands onto green paper. Cut and staple on tree branches for a leafy effect.

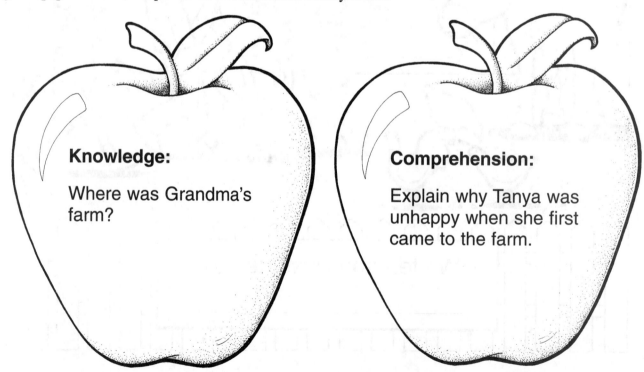

Knowledge:

Where was Grandma's farm?

Comprehension:

Explain why Tanya was unhappy when she first came to the farm.

12

An Apple a Day . . . *(cont.)*

Application:

If you were Tanya, what would you have done on the farm?

Synthesis:

Predict what might happen the next time Tanya visits the farm.

Analysis:

Why did Grandma like being on the farm?

Evaluation:

Which character in the story would you like to be? Explain why.

Bus Fare Math

Directions: Duplicate the bus and ticket pages. Cut out the bus shapes and tickets. Glue the bus shapes to a file folder and laminate the folder and tickets. Place the tickets in an envelope labeled with the name of the activity. Students are to total the amount of money found on the buses and then match the tickets to the correct buses.

14

Bus Fare Math (cont.)

Bus Fare Math *(cont.)*

Match these tickets to the correct amount of money on each bus.

55¢	**70¢**
$1.00	**$1.30**
25¢	**45¢**
60¢	**$1.65**

16

Farm Story Problems

Color, cut around the border, and glue the two halves of the farm scene together. Use the picture to solve the story problems on the worksheet.

Farm Story Problems *(cont.)*

Glue page 17 here.

18

Farm Story Problems *(cont.)*

1. There are three chickens on the farm. Each chicken laid two eggs. How many eggs are there altogether?

2. Five beautiful flowers are growing in the field. You pick three of the flowers. How many are left?

3. One apple tree has six apples. The other tree has five apples. You pick all the apples, then you eat one. How many apples are left?

4. On the farm, there are three chickens, one dog, one cat and two cows. What is the total number of animals on the farm?

5. The farmer wants to have eleven apple trees in the orchard. He now has two. How many more trees will he need to plant?

6. Two cows are standing near the barn. Each cow gives three pails of milk, but one pail spills. How many pails of milk are left?

Grandfather's Lovesong

by Reeve Lindbergh

Summary

A young boy and his grandfather express their profound and everlasting love for each another in this sensitively written patterned poetry. Reeve Lindbergh's loving verse is beautifully illustrated in soft tones by Rachel Isadora. Together the boy and his grandfather express their boundless love and explore a variety of areas in nature as seasonal changes take place.

The outline below is a suggested five-day plan for using the various activities that are presented in this unit. However, you should adapt these ideas to fit your own classroom situation.

Sample Plan

Day 1

- Read *Grandfather's Lovesong* and begin Enjoying the Book activities. (page 22)
- Complete the Seasons Mini-Book. (page 25)
- Begin Daily Writing Topics. (page 24)

Day 2

- Reread *Grandfather's Lovesong*, calling attention to the pattern used in the text.
- Discuss rhyming words in the text, following Extending the Book activities. (page 22)
- Reinforce recognition of rhyming words with the Rhyming Words activity. (page 26)
- Reinforce the poetry pattern in the text with Lovesong Innovations. (page 27)
- Read about the author in Meet Reeve Lindbergh. (page 42)
- Continue Daily Writing Topics. (page 24)

Day 3

- Practice sorting and classifying skills using the four seasons in Seasonal Sorting. (page 28)
- Identify the types of weather found in *Grandfather's Lovesong*. Research these types of weather on a weather map from your local newspaper.
- Complete Read a Weather Map. (page 29)
- Sing Grandparent Lovesongs and compose your own lovesongs set to the tune of familiar songs. (page 68)
- Continue Daily Writing Topics. (page 24)

Day 4

- Teach reasoning skills with Seasonal Logic. (page 30)
- Brainstorm a list of fun places to visit with a grandparent and write a class book, Travels With Grandfather. (page 32)
- Complete activities in A Map for Your Day With Grandfather. (page 31)
- Conduct a survey of students to find out in which type of region each would prefer to live: farm, mountain, ocean, desert, forest. Organize findings in Where Would You Like to Live? (page 46)
- Continue Daily Writing Topics. (page 24)

Day 5

- Conduct the science project, Make It Rain. (page 52)
- Record your observations in Science Observation Journal. (page 53)
- Discuss different types of precipitation and what causes each. Make and read the Precipitation Booklet. (page 54)
- Continue Daily Writing Topics. (page 24)
- Plan Grandparents' Gala culminating activity. (page 74)
- Continue Extending the Book. (page 23)

Overview of Activities

Setting the Stage

1. Prepare the classroom for the grandparent unit. Make a banner with the words Grandparents Gallery in large block letters, either by hand or using a computer program. Place this large banner in the center of a bulletin board. Have a display table at the base of the bulletin board with the sign designating this as the Family Historical Corner.

2. Discuss grandparents with your students. Do they have grandparents? How often do they see them? Do their grandparents live near them or do they live far away?

3. Brainstorm things that the children do with their grandparents. Record the students' responses on a sheet of chart paper titled What We Do With Our Grandparents and display this on the bulletin board. Children might further group these ideas into Fun Things and Helping Things. You can also display the word web from *Tanya's Reunion* to stimulate further discussion.

What We Do With Our Grandparents	
Sing	Swim
Dance	Sled
Bake	Go to the park
Watch videos	

4. If possible, take a walk outside your school to observe any seasonal changes that may be visible in your area. This will help students grasp the concept of setting in a book and changes in nature. You can also use pictures cut from old calendars that show how nature changes with the seasons; laminate these pictures to make them more durable. These pictures may be displayed on a bulletin board with the title Our Changing Seasons in your science area. This area should be supplied with informational books and posters about the four seasons for students to explore independently.

Overview of Activities *(cont.)*

Enjoying the Book

1. Introduce *Grandfather's Lovesong* to your students by discussing the cover and asking students to predict what the story might be about.

2. Then take a picture walk through the book by showing the students several of the illustrations in the book. Discuss how the setting changes from one illustration to the next (seasonal changes and changes in regional areas). Ask students to compare these settings to your area and season.

3. Read *Grandfather's Lovesong* for enjoyment. You might want to play a commercially available nature cassette tape or CD while you read the book to complement the book and help set a calm peaceful mood. Encourage students to examine the details in each illustration and discuss them.

4. Encourage students to be involved in the book and participate as active listeners. Discuss the following:

   > Do you notice a family resemblance between the boy and his grandfather? (Refer to the title page.)

   > How do the boy and Grandfather feel about each other? How can you tell?

   > What sounds might you hear on each page?

5. Challenge your students to identify the pattern used in the verse by asking questions such as "How are the words on each page alike?" and "Which words rhyme on each page?"

6. Have your students use context and illustrations to determine what a mare is (as mentioned on page 20 in the book) and what a sparrow is (as mentioned on page 30 in the book).

7. Look carefully at the scenes of nature. Identify and list the regions that are shown in the book (farm, forest, mountain, ocean, lake).

8. What seasons do you see depicted in the illustrations and text? Is there a difference in the clothing people wear in each season? Make a chart to record the seasons. What parts of the book help to identify the seasons? (Mention that fall and autumn name the same season.) Add page numbers from the book to validate your observations.

Spring	Summer	Fall (Autumn)	Winter
Warm spring air (p. 20)	Summer rain (p. 24)	Geese (p. 11) red leaves (p. 11)	Snow (p. 15)

Extending the Book

1. Look for the words that rhyme on each page of the text. List these words by word families on strips of adding machine paper. Display these in your classroom, perhaps at your reading center.

-eep	-ow	-ong	-all	-old
deep	low	song	call	cold
sleep	grow	strong	fall	gold
sheep	below	long	tall	bold

Overview of Activities *(cont.)*

Extending the Book *(cont.)*

2. Examine the pattern of the text on each page. Write the words on sentence strips and put them in a pocket chart. Work with your students to make a class innovation following the pattern. Display this as a sample to help students in creating their own innovations.

3. Discuss which months of the year may correlate with each illustration. Name the months of the year in order.

4. Encourage students to use watercolors to paint different nature scenes of several different regions (farm, mountain, ocean, lake, forest, desert). Mount the paintings on white construction paper and then add a border of gray construction paper, similar to the illustrations in the book. Students may write their own text to correlate with their paintings. These may be displayed on a bulletin board or in a class book.

5. Make a list of animals that are mentioned in the text or shown in the illustrations of *Grandfather's Lovesong*. These animals may be sorted into different groups (mammals—birds; four legs—two legs; can fly—can't fly; farm animals—animals in the wild, etc.)

6. To build knowledge, especially for students who may live in an area that does not have distinct changes from one season to the next, read informational books about the four seasons (see Bibliography for references). Add new information learned to the chart of Seasonal Signs that you started during the Enjoying the Book activities.

7. Teach the children several traditional children's songs that their grandparents may have learned as children, such as "Are You Sleeping?," "Mary Had a Little Lamb," "The Itsy Bitsy Spider," "Twinkle Twinkle Little Star," "Old MacDonald Had a Farm," "This Old Man," "A-Tisket A-Tasket, "Little Boy Blue" and "Ring Around the Rosy." Make a graph to show which of these traditional songs is the most popular with your students. Children may use rhythm instruments to accompany each of the songs and perform them at the Grandparents' Gala culminating activity.

8. Use a map of the United States (page 77) or a map of the world (page 78) to locate different locations that are farm regions, mountainous regions, ocean areas, lake areas, and desert regions. Be sure to look for Maine since it is mentioned in the text. Use the words *north*, *south*, *east*, and *west* as you locate and compare locations.

9. Use the Share a Bedtime Story with a Grandparent letter (page 43) to encourage children to spend some special time with a grandparent.

10. Learn about life when grandparents and parents were the age of your students. Read *In Grandma's Day* by Paul Humphrey and complete the Past and Present Book (page 35). Send home Who Was the President When My Grandparents and Parents Were My Age? (page 60). Make a graph to display the results.

Daily Writing Topics

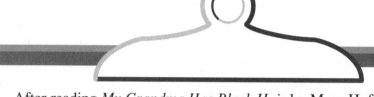

1. After reading *My Grandma Has Black Hair* by Mary Hoffman, write your own story about a modern grandma.

2. Imagine that you had spent a weekend with a grandparent. You had a terrific time! Write a thank-you note to him or her. You might want to use the stationery on page 76.

3. Pretend that you are outside on a beautiful autumn afternoon. Leaves are falling all around you. Make a list of games you might play in the colorful fall leaves. Explain the rules for playing each game.

4. You have gone to the ocean for the day. Unexpectedly, it starts to rain and the rain becomes a downpour! What would you see? Hear? Do?

5. Imagine that you went sailing in a sailboat on a lovely summer day. Where would you sail? Whom would you take with you? What supplies would you take? What would you see? Write about your adventure.

6. Write about a day during your favorite season. Tell what you do for fun.

7. Pretend that you went fishing with Grandfather at the lake. What did you use for bait? What did you catch? What did you and Grandfather talk about? Write about your fishing trip.

8. Go outside and look up into the sky. Do you see any birds? Do the clouds look like animals or unusual things? Use your imagination and write about what you see in the sky.

9. You may go anywhere in the world with your grandfather. Where would you go? Why would you go there? How would you get there? Write about your trip. Compile these stories into a class book called Travels With Grandfather. (page 32)

10. Look at the scarecrow shown on page 12 of *Grandfather's Lovesong*. Write what the scarecrow might be thinking or saying.

11. Pretend that you are spending a week on a farm. Use details to tell about your week.

12. Imagine that you are home on a dark snowy night. It snows so hard that you get snowed in! What will you do?

13. You visited a real lighthouse along the rocky shoreline. What did you see? What did you do?

14. A deer just ran across a country road and into the woods. You decide to follow it. Describe what you see. What happens in the woods?

Seasons Mini-Book

My Mini-Book About
Seasons

by _____

It gets cooler. Pumpkins and apples get ripe. Geese fly south to stay warmer.   1

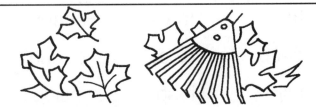

Leaves on the trees become red, yellow, and orange. They fall from the trees. This is fall.   2

It gets colder. Snow and ice fall from clouds in the sky.   3

When it snows, you can make a snowman and go sledding. This is winter.   4

It gets warmer. The snow melts. Rains come and help flowers grow. Trees grow green leaves.   5

When it rains, you will need to use an umbrella. This is spring.   6

It gets hotter. Days are longer, and the sun shines brightly.   7

Swimming helps us stay cool in the hot summer months.   8

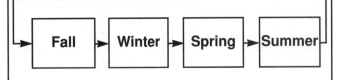

There are four seasons—fall, winter, spring, and summer.   9

Name _____

Rhyming Words

The author in *Grandfather's Lovesong* used many rhyming words to tell the story. Write the words from the Word Box into the correct columns to make word families that rhyme. Think of more words that rhyme and add your own words to each group to complete each column.

Word Box

free	call	plain	true	mare	sheep
wide	deer	fair	deep	clear	strong
gold	high	sea	tall	long	inside
grow	by	bold	view	Maine	below

fall	**me**	**tide**	**cold**	**rain**	**low**
_____	_____	_____	_____	_____	_____
_____	_____	_____	_____	_____	_____
_____	_____	_____	_____	_____	_____
_____	_____	_____	_____	_____	_____

song	**near**	**air**	**sleep**	**sky**	**through**
_____	_____	_____	_____	_____	_____
_____	_____	_____	_____	_____	_____
_____	_____	_____	_____	_____	_____

Lovesong Innovations

The author in *Grandfather's Lovesong* followed a four-line pattern throughout the book in writing the text for each page. Look at the sample below. Notice the words that rhyme and the number of syllables in each line. Then try writing your own innovations following the same pattern.

I love you free	(four syllables)
Like the birds that fly	(five syllables)
To the oak tree	(four syllables)
High above me.	(four syllables)

I love you _____

Like_____

_____

_____.

_____

I love you _____

Like_____

_____

_____.

_____

Innovations by_____

Seasonal Sorting

These seasonal sorting cards can be placed in a science center or used as a whole class assignment.

For use at a science center, color each of these seasonal signs. Mount the cards on tagboard. Cut them apart and laminate for durability. Place the cards at your science center for children to use independently.

For a whole class activity, duplicate one set of cards for each student. Students will color the seasonal cards and cut them apart. Students then sort the cards into groups of spring, summer, fall, and winter, gluing the cards onto a large piece of paper which has been divided into four sections. (This can be used as an assessment tool.)

28

Name _____

Read a Weather Map

Sometimes we need to know what the weather will be. We can use a weather map to find out. Use the weather map below to answer the questions. Then look in your local newspaper to find a weather map for today's weather. What will your weather be like today?

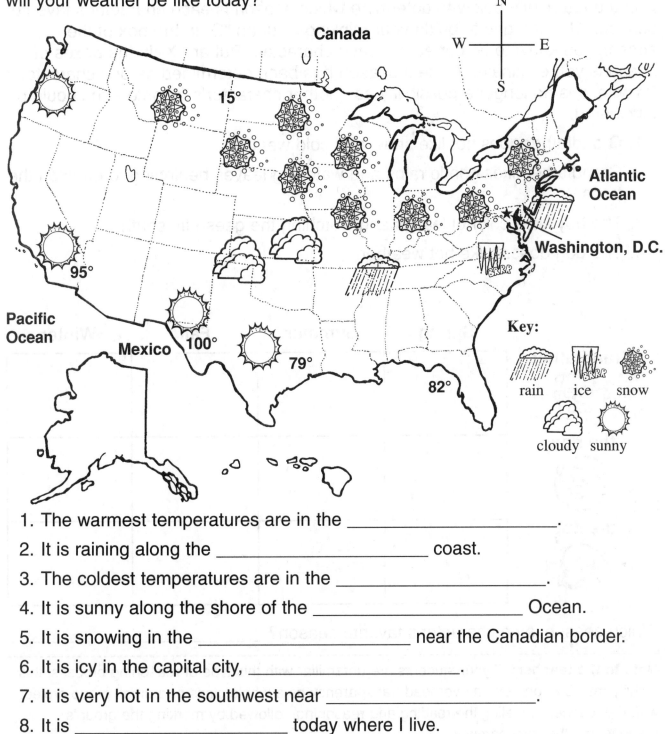

1. The warmest temperatures are in the _____.

2. It is raining along the _____ coast.

3. The coldest temperatures are in the _____.

4. It is sunny along the shore of the _____ Ocean.

5. It is snowing in the _____ near the Canadian border.

6. It is icy in the capital city, _____.

7. It is very hot in the southwest near _____.

8. It is _____ today where I live.

Seasonal Logic

Grandfather, the boy, and the dog each have a favorite season of the year. No two characters have the same favorite season. One of the four seasons is no character's favorite season.

Use the four clues below to determine which season is each character's favorite season. Use the grid to guide your thinking. Put an "O" in the box of the season you know to be correct for each character. Put an "X" in the boxes of seasons you eliminate. Once a season has been determined as one character's favorite, it is no longer a possibility as another character's favorite and should be eliminated.

1. Grandfather does not like snow and cold weather.
2. Grandfather likes gentle rains and watching leaves beginning to grow on the trees.
3. The boy likes colorful leaves and watching the geese fly south.
4. The dog doesn't like hot weather.

	Spring	Summer	Fall	Winter
Grandfather				
the boy				
the dog				

Which season is no character's favorite season? _____

- -

Note to the teacher: If your students are unfamiliar with this type of reasoning process, this activity may be done on an overhead transparency as a whole class or a small group project with the teacher modeling the reading and reasoning, followed by marking the group's response on the transparency.

Name _____

A Map for Your Day With Grandfather

Pretend that you are going to visit Grandfather. You will be spending the day with him on his farm and traveling to some of his favorite places nearby. Use the map of the area to answer the questions.

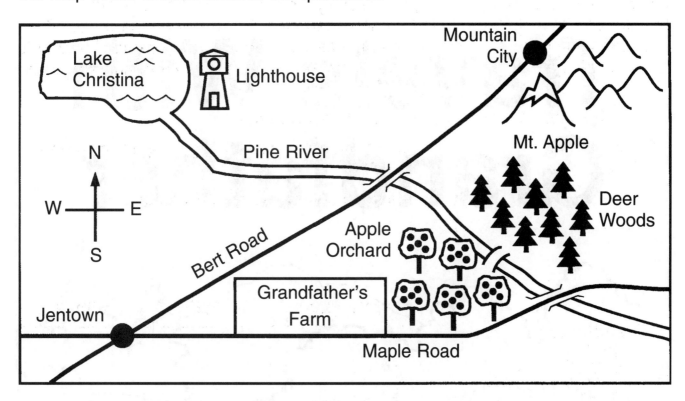

1. Grandfather's Farm is near the town called _____.

2. Lake Christina is   N   E   S   W   of Grandfather's Farm.
     (circle one)

3. Grandfather's Farm is   N   E   S   W   of his Apple Orchard.
     (circle one)

4. _____ Road runs between Jentown and Mountain City.

5. The lighthouse is on the   N   E   S   W   shore of Lake Christina.
     (circle one)

6. The Pine River is between Grandfather's Apple Orchard and
   _____.

7. Grandfather's Farm is   N   E   S   W   of Mt. Apple.
     (circle one)

Travels With Grandfather
Class Book Cover

Enlarge and reproduce the cover below on colored card stock. Cut a back cover for the class book the same size. Use markers to color the illustration, and then laminate the covers for longer use. Use metal rings or a binding machine to compile your students' stories into the class book.

Travels With Grandfather

A Class Book

By _____

32

Writing Grandparent Poetry

Cinquain

A cinquain is a poem with five lines following this form:

Line 1
>One noun which names your subject

Line 2
>Two adjectives which describe the noun

Line 3
>Three action words ending with "ing" which describe the noun

Line 4
>Four words expressing a feeling or another action

Line 5
>One word which is another word for line 1

Dad
Kind, strong
Playing, helping, loving
Cares for his child
Pal

Teaching Sequence:

1. Show an example of a cinquain poem, such as this one about a dad.
2. Choose another family member (mother, brother, etc.) and write a cinquain with the class on the chalkboard. Discuss the characteristics of each line.
3. Brainstorm words on chart paper relating the poem to grandparents.
4. Have each child write a cinquain about Grandma or Grandpa. Extension: Students can write poems about something they like to do with their grandparents (fishing, reading, etc.).

Acrostic

An acrostic is a poem in which a word or phrase is written for each letter of a word. Begin writing a grandparent acrostic by printing "GRANDMA" down the side of a piece of paper, one letter per line. Follow the same steps as above for teaching this form of poetry (show a sample, write together, etc.) Here is an example of a grandparent acrostic.

Great to be with
Ready for a hug
Always there for me
Nice to everyone
Dressed in her Sunday best
My best friend
Awesome!

Extension: For a real challenge, write acrostics that rhyme!

Grandparent Postcard

Directions: Duplicate the postcard below on white tagboard or glue it to a 5" x 8" (13 cm x 20 cm) index card, white or colored. Write a postcard to Grandma and Grandpa. Tell them why they are special or thank them for being great grandparents! On the other side of the postcard, students will draw a picture of themselves with their grandparents, perhaps doing a favorite activity. Add a stamp and mail the cards or deliver them in person when grandparents visit your classroom.

_____
Date

Dear _____,

_____

_____

_____

_____

Love,

_____

Stamp

_____

_____

_____

_____

Past and Present Book

As a prewriting activity for this book, students will interview one of their grandparents or ask for their parents' help to find out what their grandparents were like when they were children. The students will illustrate each page to match the sentences. To make the book, cut on the dotted lines and staple the left of each page. This book could also be a project that grandparent and grandchild work on together at the Gala.

Past and Present

My grandparent's favorite song was

_____.

My favorite song is

_____.

1.

Past and Present Book *(cont.)*

My grandparent's favorite school activity was _____

_____ .

My favorite school activity is _____

_____ .

2.

My grandparent liked to play _____

_____ .

I like to play _____

_____ .

3.

Past and Present Book *(cont.)*

My grandparent had _____ _____ for a pet.	I have or would like to have a pet _____ . 4.
My grandparent's favorite food was _____ .	My favorite food is _____ _____ . 5.

Past and Present Book *(cont.)*

My grandparent's favorite sport was

_____ .

My favorite sport is _____

_____ .

6.

My grandparent got to school by

_____ .

I get to school by _____

_____ .

7.

Grandparent Words

Enlarge, color, and laminate this chart to display in your writing center for students to use as a word bank when writing about grandparents and families. (This chart may also be duplicated for students to have their own individual copies.)

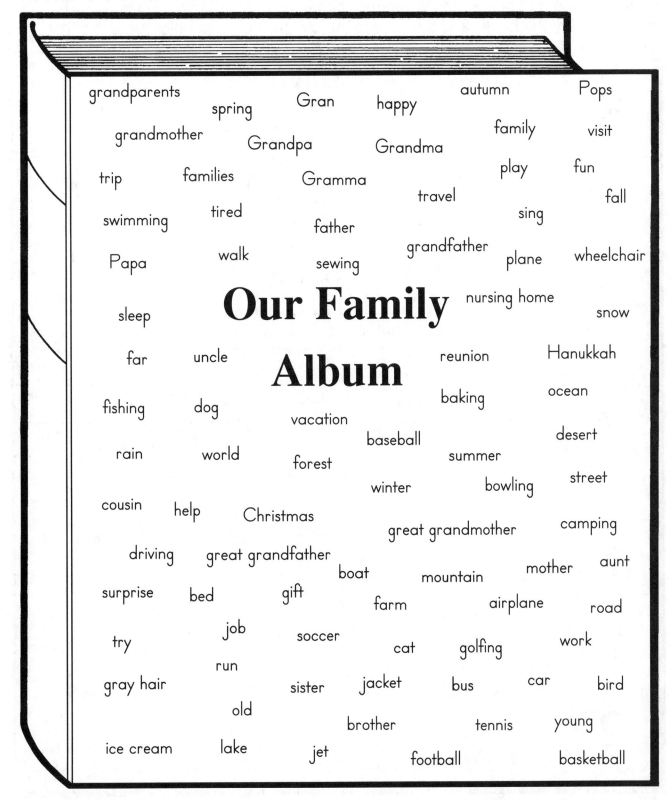

grandparents   spring   Gran   happy   autumn   Pops

grandmother   Grandpa   Grandma   family   visit

trip   families   Gramma   play   fun

swimming   tired   travel   sing   fall

Papa   walk   father   grandfather   plane   wheelchair

sewing

sleep   nursing home   snow

Our Family Album

far   uncle   reunion   Hanukkah

fishing   dog   baking   ocean

rain   world   vacation   desert

forest   baseball   summer

winter   bowling   street

cousin   help   Christmas

great grandmother   camping

driving   great grandfather

boat   mountain   mother   aunt

surprise   bed   gift   farm   airplane   road

try   job   soccer   cat   golfing   work

run

gray hair   sister   jacket   bus   car   bird

old

brother   tennis   young

ice cream   lake   jet   football   basketball

Story Summary

After reading a selected book, use the following format to summarize the story and its plot. Suitable books include *The Patchwork Quilt* and *Tanya's Reunion* by Valerie Flournoy, *Bringing the Farmhouse Home* by Gloria Whelan, and *Family Farm* by Thomas Locker. Many other books would be suitable, so choose a favorite, enjoy the book, and then complete the summary to help remember it.

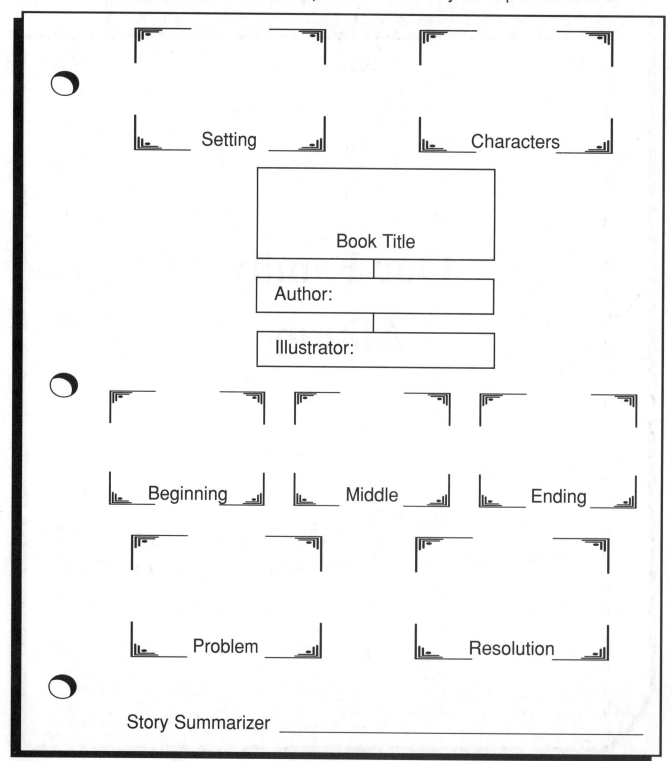

Setting

Characters

Book Title

Author:

Illustrator:

Beginning

Middle

Ending

Problem

Resolution

Story Summarizer _____

Name _____

Meet Valerie Flournoy

Valerie Flournoy is an author. She likes to write. She writes about families. She has a twin sister named Vanessa. Valerie Flournoy lives in New Jersey.

Valerie Flournoy wrote *Tanya's Reunion*. It tells about her first visit to a relative's farm when she was a little girl.

Tanya's Reunion is a sequel to her book, *The Patchwork Quilt*. A sequel is a book that tells more about the same characters in an original book. Find *The Patchwork Quilt* in your library. Read it to learn more about Tanya and her grandmother. Check out more Valerie Flournoy books and pick your favorite!

Draw a picture of Tanya and her grandmother.

Name _____

Meet Reeve Lindbergh

Reeve Lindbergh is an author. She likes to write in rhyme. She told stories for her own children, and now she writes the stories down to share with us. She lives on a farm in Vermont.

Reeve Lindbergh wrote *Grandfather's Lovesong*. She likes nature and animals. Her books have both nature and animals in them.

Two of her other books are *The Midnight Farm* and *Benjamin's Barn*. See if you can find these in your library. Then enjoy reading them, too!

Draw a picture showing your favorite scene from one of Reeve Lindbergh's books. Include the title of the book, too.

This scene is from the book entitled

_____

by Reeve Lindbergh.

Share a Bedtime Story With a Grandparent

To encourage your students to share some special quality time with a grandparent, use a Grandparent Tote. Choose a favorite children's book, such as *Goodnight Moon* by Margaret Wise Brown. Put a copy of the book into a medium-sized tote bag or child's backpack. For added fun, also include a small stuffed animal that correlates with the book, such as the bunny from *Goodnight Moon*. (A book and bunny set is commercially available.) Also include a copy of the note below and the Reading Response Page from page 44 into the tote. This will explain the activity to the grandparent and provide the child with a project to work on with the grandparent after reading the book together. Send the tote home on a rotating basis with each child in your class, or make several totes to have more than one circulating at a time. (You might make several totes, with each one having a different book.)

Date

Dear Grandparent,

Your grandchild is looking forward to spending some special time with you. Enclosed in this "Grandparent Tote" is a book that you may read to your grandchild. It is a favorite with our class. We hope you'll enjoy looking at the illustrations and talking about them as you read the book.

After you have read through the book several times your grandchild may even notice some words in the book that he or she knows and wants to read along with you. What a terrific chance to practice some beginning reading skills!

To conclude this project, please help your grandchild complete the attached Reading Response Page. Thanks so much for your help with this project and for sharing your time with such a special young person!

Sincerely,

Share a Bedtime Story with a Grandparent *(cont.)*

Reading Response Page

My grandparent and I read the book _____

_____.

It was written by _____.

It was illustrated by _____.

We liked this book because _____

_____.

Our favorite part of the book was _____

_____.

Here is a picture of our favorite part of the book.

This page was completed by _____ and

(child's name)

_____ on _____.

(grandparent's name)   (date)

Name _____

Grandparent Word Problems

Pretend that you are helping your grandparents with chores around the house. Read the information given in each problem. Use addition or subtraction to find the answers to the questions.

1. You need to help your grandpa rake the leaves in his yard. There are eight trees in his backyard and four trees in his front yard. How many more trees are in the backyard than in the front yard? _____ trees

2. You and your grandma are working in her garden. You see six red tulips and three yellow tulips. How many tulips do you see altogether? _____ tulips

3. You and your grandmother are pulling up weeds around the house. There are ten weeds altogether. Your grandmother pulled up five of the weeds and went inside to rest. How many weeds do you need to pull up to finish the job? _____ weeds

4. Your grandfather was cleaning out the mitten box. He found six pairs of mittens. How many mittens did he find altogether? _____ mittens

5. You have worked hard helping your grandparents, so you have gone on a fishing trip with them to relax. Grandma caught four fish. Grandpa caught half as many as Grandma. How many fish did Grandpa catch? _____ fish

6. After fishing, Grandpa treats all of you to ice cream cones. Grandpa has 3 scoops of ice cream in his cone. Grandma has two scoops of ice cream in her cone. You get four scoops of ice cream in your cone. How many scoops of ice cream did the three of you get altogether? _____ scoops of ice cream

Graphing Grandparent Activities

Graphs are an important part of a primary math curriculum, and can be incorporated into the Grandparent Unit in a variety of ways.

Begin by constructing a permanent graph that can be mounted on the board or a chart rack and used repeatedly in your classroom. On a large sheet of tagboard, draw vertical and horizontal lines with a permanent black marker, leaving space to write in information on the left side and the bottom. The graph can be used both horizontally and vertically. You can also use plastic or electrical tape to make the grid. Laminate the tagboard after drawing the lines. Do not label until after it is laminated. To use, write names, headings, bars, or numbers on the graph with an overhead marker. After each use, wipe off with water and a paper towel.

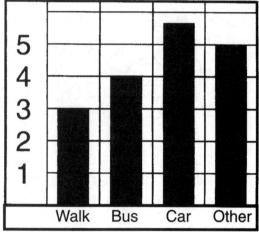

Discuss results with students at the conclusion of each graphing activity, incorporating appropriate math terminology such as greater than, less than, most, least, the difference between, the total of, etc.

This permanent graph can be used as a bar graph or you can have students add a symbol of their choice. Reproducible symbols for these graphs follow on page 47.

Grandparent Graphs

Family Travels (To be used with *Tanya's Reunion*)
How do you travel to your grandparent's house? Complete the graph to find out how students get to grandma's or grandpa's for a visit.

Walk	Bus	Train	Airplane	Car	Other

Where Would You Like to Live? (To be used with *Grandfather's Lovesong*)
Conduct a survey of the students in your class to determine which region is the most popular to live. Use your findings to complete the graph.

Farm	Mountain	Ocean	Lake	Forest	Desert

Graph Your Favorite Farm Animal (To be used with *Tanya's Reunion*)
Do a survey of the students in your class to find out which farm animal is each student's favorite. Use your findings to complete the graph.

Cow	Pig	Sheep	Chicken	Horse	Goat	Duck	Goose	Turkey	Other

Graphing Grandparent Activities *(cont.)*

These reproducible symbols are for use with the graphing activities on the previous page.

Name _____

Past and Present Calculator Math

Prices on basic items have changed since your grandparents were your age. Use the Past and Present Price Lists below to calculate the answers to the following questions. Use a calculator to determine the answers.

Past Price List

gallon of milk . . . . $.80
loaf of bread. . . . . $.12
box of cereal . . . . $.27
soda pop . . . . $.05
bicycle $44.95
baseball $2.35
pair of socks . . . . $.35
toothpaste . . . . $.37

Present Price List

gallon of milk $2.19
loaf of bread. $1.27
box of cereal $3.89
soda pop . . . . $.75
bicycle $109.00
baseball $12.00
pair of socks $1.30
toothpaste $2.33

1. How much more does a soda pop cost now than it did in the past?_____

2. How much less did a baseball cost in the past than it does now?_____

3. If you went to the store now to buy milk, bread, and cereal now, how much would it cost?_____

4. If you went to the store in the past to buy milk, bread, and cereal, how much would it cost?_____

5. Compare your answers in #3 and #4. How much more does it cost now to buy these three items than it did in the past?_____

6. How much less did a bicycle cost in the past than it does now?

_____

Bonus Questions:

1. What is the total amount of money needed to purchase all of the items on the Past Price List?_____

2. What is the total amount of money needed to purchase all of the items on the Present Price List?_____

3. What is the difference between the totals on the Past Price List and the Present Price List?_____

Note: Prices from the past were taken from the section called "*Selected Prices—1945—1949*" in *The Value of a Dollar: Prices and Incomes in the U.S.*, edited by Scott Derks. Prices for the present were accurate on a random sampling of items in Midland, Michigan, as of July 1996.

Domino Math

Duplicate this page. Color the dominoes on the page. Mount the page on tagboard, and cut out the individual dominoes. Laminate the dominoes to make them more durable. You could decorate the back of each domino before laminating it, or you could cover the back of each with decorative self-adhesive vinyl after laminating. Give each student two different dominoes. Use the dominoes to do Domino Math on page 50 to practice number families. Make an overhead transparency of page 50 to introduce and model this strategy to your students. Students may work in pairs to check each other's work.

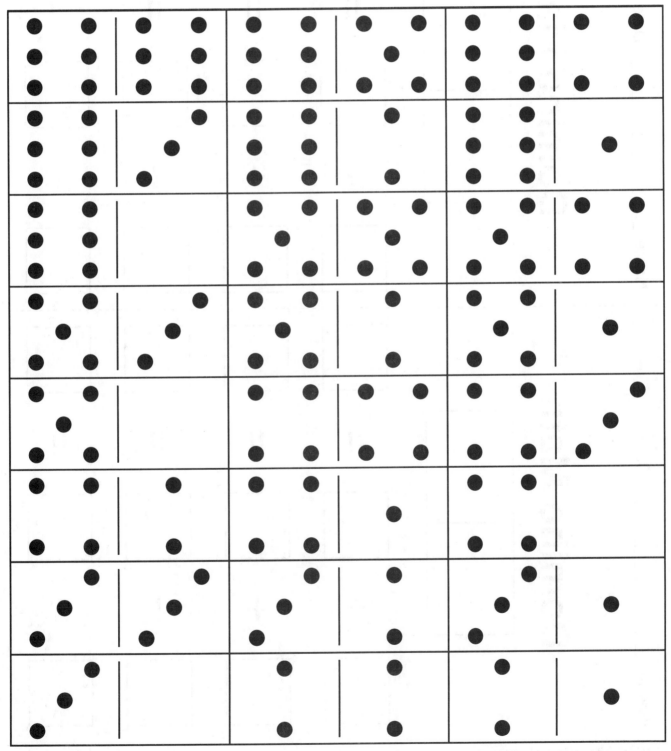

Domino Math *(cont.)*

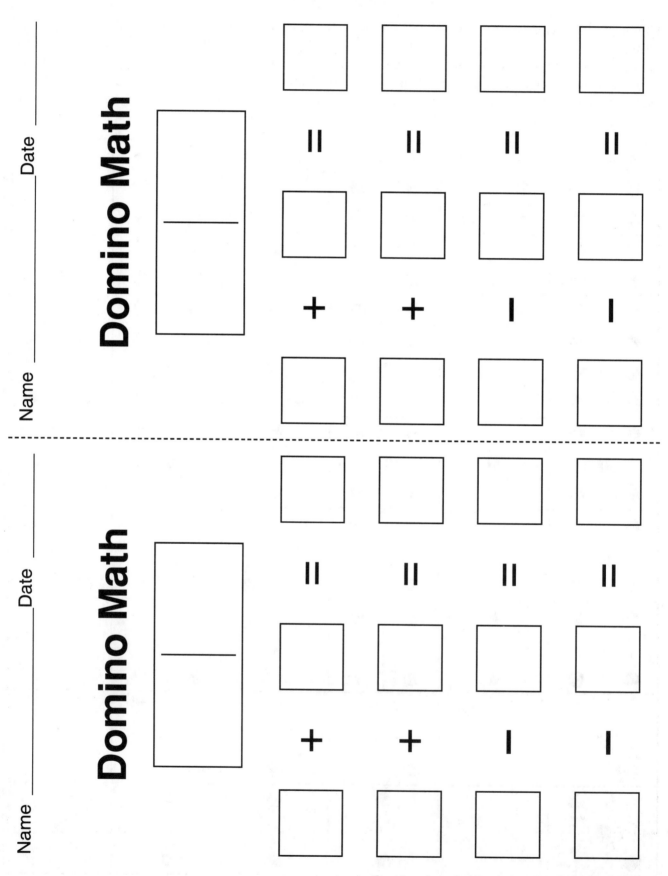

Pattern Quilt

Quilts often use a pattern of colors and shapes to create a beautiful design. Use the grid below to make a new quilt design. A simple pattern may be made by coloring the squares (red, yellow, blue, red, yellow, etc.). A more complex pattern can be created by dividing the squares diagonally before coloring.

Make It Rain

Expected Outcome:
Students will observe the process by which raindrops are formed and record their observations in a Science Observation Journal.

Question to guide experiment:
How do raindrops form?

Materials:
- ☐ teakettle
- ☐ water
- ☐ hot plate
- ☐ metal cake pan (9" x 13"/ 23 cm x 33 cm)
- ☐ ice cubes
- ☐ live green plant (optional)
- ☐ Science Observation Journal (page 53) for each student

Procedure:

1. Gather all materials on a table so students can easily observe the experiment as you perform it. Assemble your students seated around you so they are not tempted to crowd too close to the heat source. Explain that today you will be doing an experiment to see if you can make it rain in your classroom, but on a very small scale. Caution students to stay back from the hot plate, because it will get very hot during the experiment. Explain that a heat source is needed in the real water cycle. Compare the hot plate to the sun as a heat source. Include terminology in your demonstration such as *evaporation, condensation, precipitation,* and *accumulation.*

2. Fill the teakettle about two-thirds full with water, put the teakettle on the hot plate, and turn it on. You can pre-heat the water so you don't waste time during the demonstration. Compare the water in the teakettle to real bodies of water, such as a lake, the ocean, or a puddle on the street. They all evaporate into the atmosphere.

3. Fill the metal cake pan with ice cubes. This represents the cooler temperatures at cloud level. Hold this metal pan over the spout of the teakettle when the water in the teakettle starts boiling.

4. Observe that as the water in the teakettle boils and steam begins to come out of the spout, it travels up into the air as water vapor. The vapor condenses on the bottom of the pan like water droplets collecting in a cloud. When too much condensation collects, water droplets will fall like rain. You can create a good visual effect by placing the live plant where the droplets are falling, so that the "rain" will water the plant. Ask students if they know other forms of precipitation (rain, snow, hail, sleet). Enforce the concept of "cycle" as something that goes around over and over again. This experiment is an excellent opportunity to observe water in its three states: liquid, vapor or gas, and solid.

5. Have children record their observations in their Science Observation Journal.

52

Science Observation Journal

Duplicate the sheet below for each student. Cut along the solid lines, and fold along the dotted lines as shown. Then record observations as directed.

3

Here is a picture of what I observed.

2

This is what happened.

This is what I learned.

Science Observation Journal

4

_____
(Name)

Precipitation Booklet

Cut along the solid lines, put the pages in the correct order, and then staple to make a booklet. Read your Precipitation Booklet, then color the pictures.

My Precipitation Booklet

_____

(Name)

Precipitation is water that falls from clouds as rain, snow, sleet, or hail.

2

When water droplets fall from the sky, we call it rain. We need rain so that trees, grass, fruits, vegetables, and flowers can grow.

3

Sometimes tiny frozen crystals fall from the sky as white, six-sided flakes. We call this snow. When it snows a lot, we call it a blizzard.

4

Sometimes rain and snow both fall during the same storm. When this happens, we call it sleet. It makes roads icy and slippery.

5

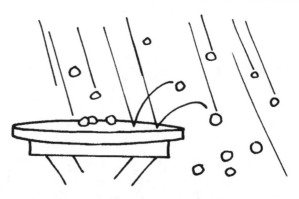

Sometimes raindrops freeze into balls of ice before they hit the ground. We call this hail.

6

54

Weather Picture Graph

Observe the weather in your area for one month. Each day make the corresponding symbol in the box that best describes the weather for the day. At the end of the month, you will have a complete weather record.

Sunny = ☀ Cloudy = ☁

Rainy  = ◌◌◌ Foggy = ▨

Windy = ≋ Snowy = ✳✳

_____
Month

Sunny	Rainy	Windy	Cloudy	Foggy	Snowy

Note to Teachers: This can be done in the classroom or sent home as a homework assignment. After completing the picture graph, ask each student to explain what information the graph shows or to write an explanation of the graph in a math journal. Encourage terminology such as "more" and "less," in addition to a variety of comparison statements. This can be one means of assessing your students' understanding of graphs.

Farm Animal Research Booklet

Choose a farm animal that you would like to learn more about. Use resource materials to find information about the animal. Record the information on the appropriate barn shape. Then cut out each barn, put them in the correct order, and staple them together to make a barn shape booklet.

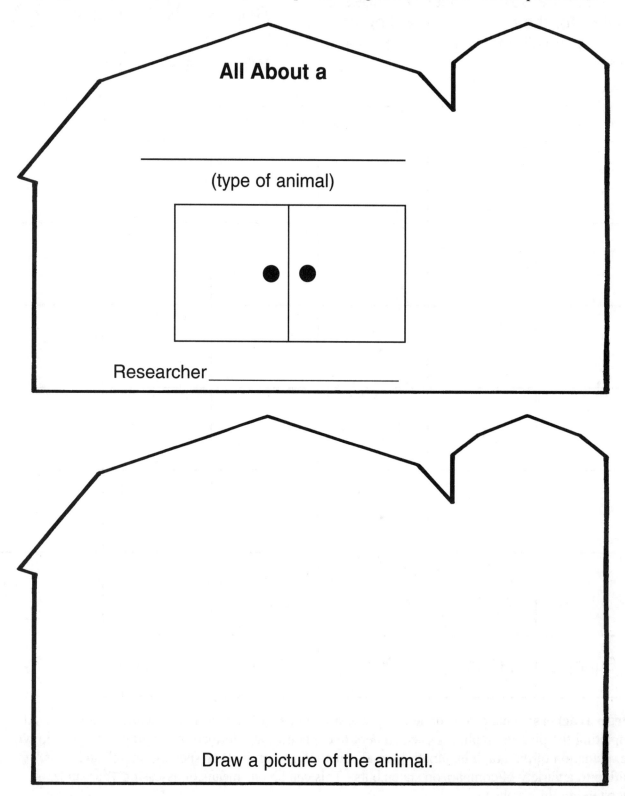

All About a

_____

(type of animal)

Researcher_____

Draw a picture of the animal.

Farm Animal Research Booklet *(cont.)*

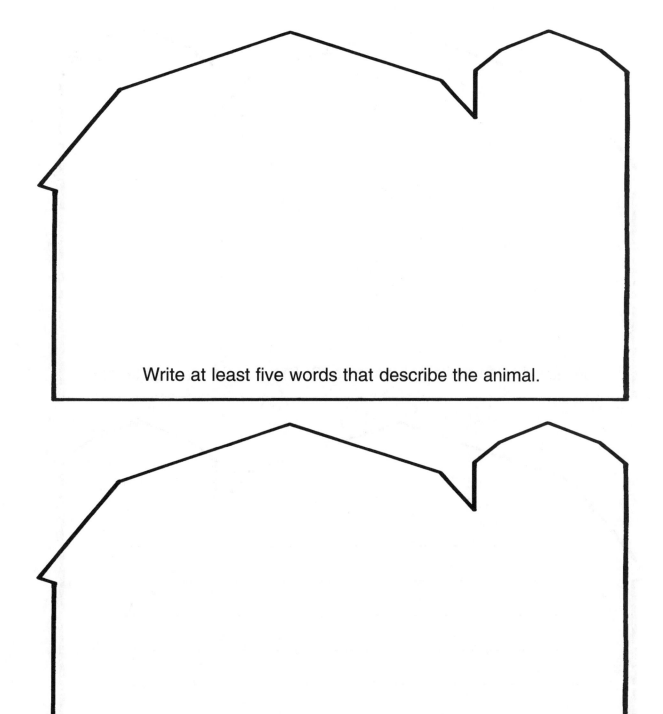

Write at least five words that describe the animal.

What does this animal eat? Draw a picture and label it.

Farm Animal Research Booklet *(cont.)*

What are this animal's babies called? Draw a picture and label it.

Write at least three other facts you learned about this animal.

58

Family Historical Corner

Families often save items which reflect their personal history. Photograph albums, scrapbooks, baby books, and portraits preserve memories of family members past and present. Handmade quilts and wedding gowns may be passed down from one generation to another. Having a historical corner in the classroom will help students to understand the importance of studying and treasuring their family's heritage.

Teacher Preparation: Choose an area of the classroom for the historical corner. Have students make and decorate a large sign or banner for the corner. You will need a large table for displaying objects that are brought in by the students.

Invite grandparents to send in antiques or items from their childhood. In addition, have the students bring in "antiques" or mementos from when they were babies or toddlers. Possible ideas might include baby blankets, bonnets, a favorite toy, book, rattle, or a favorite stuffed animal or doll.

Explain to the students that historical displays in museums usually have a descriptive label or sign with information about each item. Duplicate and have each student complete the label provided below to display with his or her contribution to the history corner.

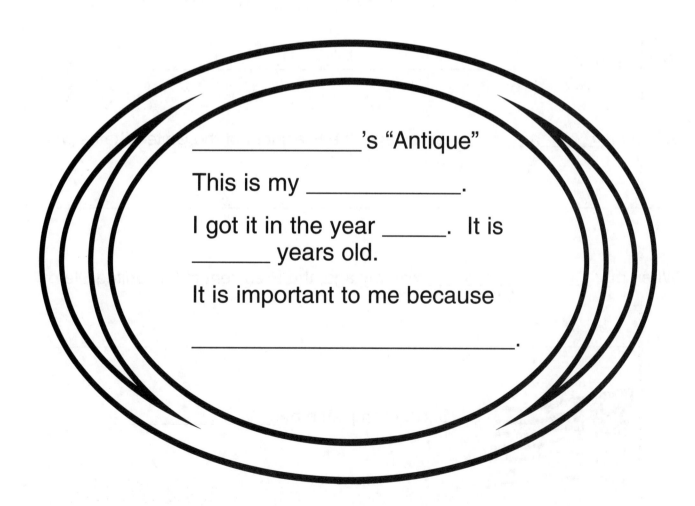

_____'s "Antique"

This is my _____.

I got it in the year _____. It is _____ years old.

It is important to me because

_____.

Who Was President When My Grandparents and Parents Were My Age?

This activity would correlate with a unit about the Presidents of the United States, as well as grandparents. Read an informational book, such as *The Buck Stops Here* by Alice Provensen. Then send home the survey below to help history become more real for your students. Include a note to parents and grandparents explaining the purpose of this homework assignment and giving them a due date. Make a graph to display the results of your survey, as explained on page 61.

Who Was President?

I am _____ years old. I am in grade _____. The President of the United

States now is _____.

When my _____ was my age, the President of the United States was
         (parent)

_____.

When my _____ was my age, the President of the United States
        (grandparent)

was _____.

Survey completed by _____.

Who Was President When My Grandparents and Parents Were My Age? *(cont.)*

Enlarge this list of United States Presidents and mount it on a large piece of blue bulletin board paper. Cut two stars out of white construction paper for each student. Put a "G" on one of each students' white stars to denote "Grandparent." Put a "P" on the other of each students' white stars to denote "Parent." Use the results of the survey to glue the stars next to the names of the appropriate presidents. Put a picture of your entire class next to the name of the current president. Laminate the graph before attaching the stars to make it useful for more than one year.

Presidents of the United States

George Washington 1789–1797

John Adams 1797–1801

Thomas Jefferson 1801–1809

James Madison 1809–1817

James Monroe 1817–1825

John Quincy Adams 1825–1829

Andrew Jackson 1829–1837

Martin Van Buren 1837–1841

William Henry Harrison 1841

John Tyler 1841–1845

James K. Polk 1845–1849

Zachary Taylor 1849–1850

Millard Fillmore 1850–1853

Franklin Pierce 1853–1857

James Buchanan 1857–1861

Abraham Lincoln 1861–1865

Andrew Johnson 1865–1869

Ulysses S. Grant 1869–1877

Rutherford B. Hayes 1877–1881

James Garfield 1881

Chester A. Arthur 1881–1885

Grover Cleveland 1885–1889, 1893–1897

Benjamin Harrison 1889–1893

William McKinley 1897–1901

Theodore Roosevelt 1901–1909

William H. Taft 1909–1913

Woodrow Wilson 1913–1921

Warren G. Harding 1921–1923

Calvin Coolidge 1923–1929

Herbert Hoover 1929–1933

Franklin D. Roosevelt 1933–1945

Harry S. Truman 1945–1953

Dwight D. Eisenhower 1953–1961

John F. Kennedy 1961–1963

Lyndon B. Johnson 1963–1969

Richard M. Nixon 1969–1974

Gerald Ford 1974–1977

Jimmy Carter 1977–1981

Ronald Reagan 1981–1989

George Bush 1989–1993

Bill Clinton 1993–

Family Quilt Letter

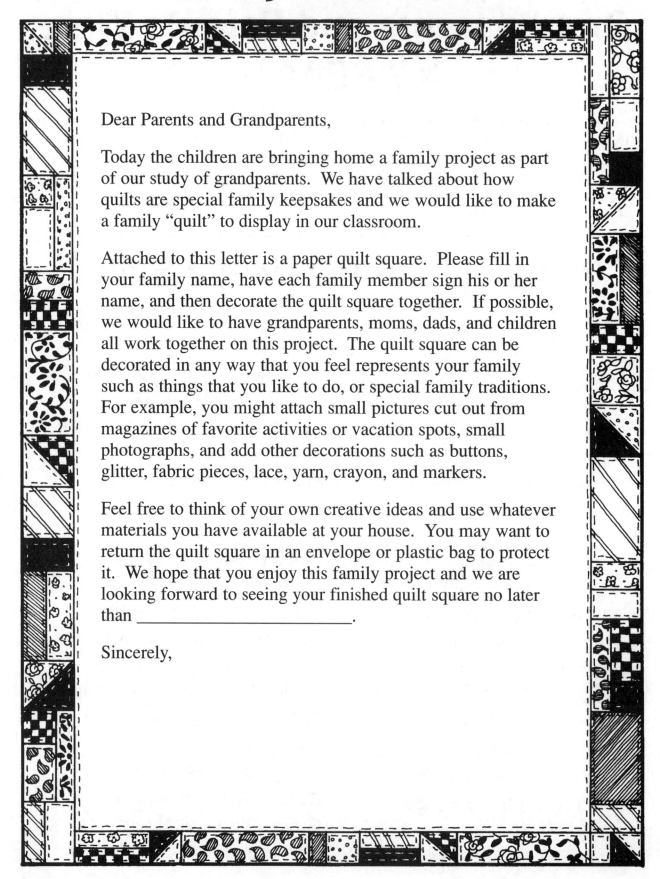

Dear Parents and Grandparents,

Today the children are bringing home a family project as part of our study of grandparents. We have talked about how quilts are special family keepsakes and we would like to make a family "quilt" to display in our classroom.

Attached to this letter is a paper quilt square. Please fill in your family name, have each family member sign his or her name, and then decorate the quilt square together. If possible, we would like to have grandparents, moms, dads, and children all work together on this project. The quilt square can be decorated in any way that you feel represents your family such as things that you like to do, or special family traditions. For example, you might attach small pictures cut out from magazines of favorite activities or vacation spots, small photographs, and add other decorations such as buttons, glitter, fabric pieces, lace, yarn, crayon, and markers.

Feel free to think of your own creative ideas and use whatever materials you have available at your house. You may want to return the quilt square in an envelope or plastic bag to protect it. We hope that you enjoy this family project and we are looking forward to seeing your finished quilt square no later than _____.

Sincerely,

Family Quilt Square

The

_____

Family

Grandparent Cards

Duplicate a card for each student. The cards may be colored and decorated with markers, crayons, color pencils, glitter, and stickers. Students are to write a message to their grandparents inside the card.

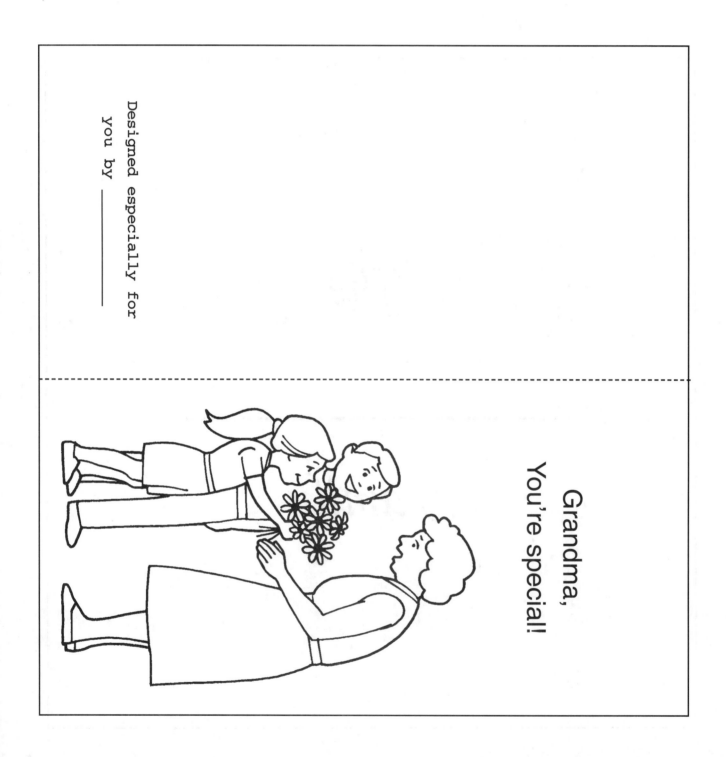

Grandparent Cards *(cont.)*

Designed especially for
you by _____

I Love You
Grandpa!

Grandparent Puzzle

Duplicate the puzzle on white tagboard or construction paper. Have the students color the picture and cut it apart on the lines. Put the puzzle pieces in an envelope and have the children reassemble the puzzle with their grandparents' help at the Grandparents' Gala. (See page 74.)

More Art Ideas

Heart Art

Cut 8" (20 cm) heart shapes out of red or pink construction paper. Have each student dip a hand in a shallow container of white tempera paint (add a few drops of dishwashing liquid to help in cleanup). Each student makes a handprint by pressing his or her hand firmly in the center of the heart. On the border of the hearts students will print the words, "My heart belongs to _____. These handprint hearts make a nice gift or may be used as a display with the title "Our Hearts Belong to Our Grandparents" at the Grandparent's Gala culminating activity!

Simple Sachets

Make a sachet for grandparents to take home as a keepsake. Cut 5" (13 cm) squares of cloth in a variety of colors and patterns. Use pinking shears to cut the cloth to prevent unraveling. Place about 2 tablespoons (30 ml) of potpourri in the center of each square. Gather up the sides and tie with yarn or ribbon.

Slate Sayings

In one room schoolhouses of the past, children did their work on chalk slates. Try making these paper slates for an "old-fashioned" project. First, cut construction paper in the following shapes.

Black construction paper	5" x 7" (13 cm x 18 cm) rectangles
Brown construction paper	1" x 5" (2.54 cm x 13 cm) strips
	1" x 7" (2.54 x 18 cm) strips

Each student will need four brown strips (2 of each size) and one black rectangle. To make the slate, glue the brown strips on the edges of the black paper. Cut some brown twine or string (about 10" or 25 cm) and glue it to the top corners of the slate to form a hanger. Have the children choose a saying to copy on their slates. The sayings can be printed using a white crayon or chalk.

Examples:

A penny saved is a penny earned.

An apple a day keeps the doctor away.

Pretty is as pretty does.

One good turn deserves another.

Do unto others as you would have others do unto you.

Grandparent Lovesongs

Use the tunes of familiar songs to create your own lovesongs for grandparents. Songs such as "Are You Sleeping?" "Mary Had a Little Lamb," "Old MacDonald Had a Farm," and "The Farmer in the Dell" provide basic melodies that can be used to create suitable lovesongs by writing your own original lines to fit the melodies.

Here is a sample to get your started. It might be performed at the Grandparents' Gala culminating activity, as described on page 74.

"I Love You"
(Sung to the tune "Are You Sleeping")

I love grandma.
I love grandma.
Yes, I do.
Yes, I do.
She is very special.
She is very special.
Yes, it's true.
Yes, it's true.

I love grandpa.
I love grandpa.
Yes, I do.
Yes, I do.
He is very special.
He is very special.
Yes, it's true.
Yes, it's true.

Create your own original Grandparent Lovesong.

_____

_____

_____

_____

_____

_____

(Sung to the tune of " _____ ")

Words by _____

"Tanya's Grandma Had a Farm"

This song would be a good follow-up after reading *Tanya's Reunion*. Using a familiar tune, students will be reading words that were introduced in the book and using the words to sing about the book.

The words could be written on sentence strips and placed in a pocket chart at your reading center for students to read independently. The song could be presented as on overhead transparency and then duplicated for students to include in their individual poetry/song notebooks. Your students might also sing it at the Grandparents' Gala culminating activity described on page 74.

"Tanya's Grandma Had a Farm"

(Sung to the tune "Old MacDonald Had a Farm")

Tanya's grandma had a farm in Virginia.
And on that farm she had an orchard in Virginia.
With an apple here and an apple there.
Here an apple, there an apple,
Everywhere an apple-apple.
Tanya's grandma had a farm in Virginia.

Tanya's grandma had a farm in Virginia.
And on that farm she had a chicken in Virginia.
With a cluck-cluck here and a cluck-cluck there.
Here a cluck, there a cluck,
Everywhere a cluck-cluck.
Tanya's grandma had a farm in Virginia.

Tanya's grandma had a farm in Virginia.
And on that farm she had a cow in Virginia.
With a moo-moo here and a moo-moo there.
Here a moo, there a moo,
Everywhere a moo-moo.
Tanya's grandma had a farm in Virginia.

Tanya's grandma had a farm in Virginia.
And on that farm she had a family in Virginia.
With a hug-hug here and a hug-hug there.
Here a hug, there a hug,
Everywhere a hug-hug.
Tanya's grandma had a farm in Virginia!

"Sing a Song of Seasons"

The following song is a good way to reinforce the science concepts about the four seasons that your students have read about in the book, *Grandfather's Lovesong*. Music also makes it fun!

"Sing a Song of Seasons"

(Sung to the tune "Are You Sleeping?")

In the springtime,
In the springtime,
Flowers bloom,
Flowers bloom.
Spring is a season,
A very blooming season.
Springtime, springtime.

In the summer,
In the summer,
It's vacation time,
It's vacation time.
Summer is a season,
A very hot season.
Summertime, summertime.

In the autumn,
In the autumn,
Leaves fall down,
Leaves fall down.
Autumn is a season,
A very colorful season.
Autumn time, autumn time.

In the winter,
In the winter,
Snowflakes fly,
Snowflakes fly.
Winter is a season,
A very cold season.
Wintertime, wintertime.

Baking Day Recipes

In *Tanya's Reunion*, Tanya and her grandmother made many delicious treats on baking day. Try these easy recipes and have a classroom cooking day.

Apple Crisp Cups

Ingredients

- 1 cup (236 mL) crushed cinnamon graham crackers
- 6 tablespoons (90 mL) dark brown sugar
- 3 tablespoons (45 mL) soft butter or margarine
- 20 oz. (567 gm) can of apple pie filling
- foil cupcake papers
- raisins (optional)

Directions

Preheat oven to 375 F° (190° C). Line cupcake tins with foil cupcake papers. Mix the first three ingredients until a crumbly mixture is formed. Set aside. Put the apple pie filling in a bowl. Cut the apples into bite size pieces. Mix the crushed graham crackers with the brown sugar and cut in the butter with two dull knives. Spoon 2 tablespoons (30 mL) of pie filling into each paper. Top with 1 tablespoon (15 mL) of the graham cracker mixture. The crisps can also be made by layering the ingredients (apples, topping, apples, topping). Raisins may be added to the apple layer if desired. Bake for 10-12 minutes or until the apple filling is warm and the topping is slightly brown. This recipe makes approximately 16–18 mini crisps.

Mini-PBJ Sandwiches

Ingredients

- peanut butter
- jelly or jam
- bread

Materials

- cookie cutters

Here is a quick and easy "no-bake" recipe that's always a favorite with children. (**Note:** Be sure to check for food allergies in your class before using recipes with peanuts or peanut butter).

Directions:

Make a peanut butter and jelly sandwich. Find some small cookie cutters in a variety of shapes (star, heart, flower, etc.). Carefully press the cookie cutters into the middle part of the bread to cut out a mini-sandwich. Each sandwich will yield 1-2 mini-sandwiches, depending on the size of the cookie cutters. Children may eat the "leftovers" or you might place the scraps outdoors as a treat for the birds.

Family Favorite Recipes

Dear Grandparents and Parents,

Our class is planning to publish a cookbook of family favorite recipes. Could you help us by sending a recipe that your family enjoys? We would like to have all the recipes by _____ .
When all recipes have been received, a copy of the cookbook will be sent home to each family.

Thanks for your help!

Sincerely,

The Family Chefs of Room_____

_____
Date

A Recipe From The Kitchen of_____

Recipe Name: _____

Ingredients:_____

_____

_____

Directions:_____

_____

_____

_____

_____

_____

_____

_____

_____

_____

"Old Fashioned" Games

There are many games of long ago that children still play today. Try some of these "old fashioned" games during your gym or recess time.

Packing Grandma's Suitcase

This is a relay race variation of the popular word game which begins "I packed my suitcase to go to Grandma's and I took. . . "

Directions: Divide the class into four teams or squads with an equal number of children on each team. If teams are unequal, the teams with less members can have someone on the team take two turns. Tape four paper X's on the floor evenly spaced along the route the children are to run. On each X, place an item to be "packed" for the trip to Grandma's. Some suggestions are pajamas, a teddy bear, a toothbrush, and a bedtime story. The first child in each team is handed a small suitcase or totebag. When you say GO, the first person in each team runs to each X, packs the item in the bag or suitcase, runs to the finish line, which could be marked with another X or an orange plastic cone, and runs back to the next team member with the packed bag. The second person in line unpacks the bag, putting the items back on the X's. The third person would repack the bag, and so on. The race continues until one team has completed the relay.

Racing Fun

Try some races which are popular at picnics and field days, such as sack races and three legged races.

Directions: For both races, children need to be divided into four or five teams as described above. For the sack race, you will need a sturdy burlap bag large enough for a child to fit in comfortably. Children get in the sack, holding the top edge with their hands, and hop to the finish line.

For the three legged race, each child will need a partner. The partners stand side by side with their arms around each other's shoulders for extra support. Their two inner legs are tied together gently with a scarf or an elastic band. The children then try to walk to the finish line using their "three" legs.

More Ideas

Be sure to try jump roping, hopscotch, Red Rover, and other favorite childhood games. For more ideas, see *Games of Long Ago* by Bobbie Kalman (bibliography, page 79).

Grandparents' Gala

Children enjoy having grandparents visit the classroom. To end this unit on grandparents with a special celebration, use some or all of these ideas to plan a Grandparents' Gala.

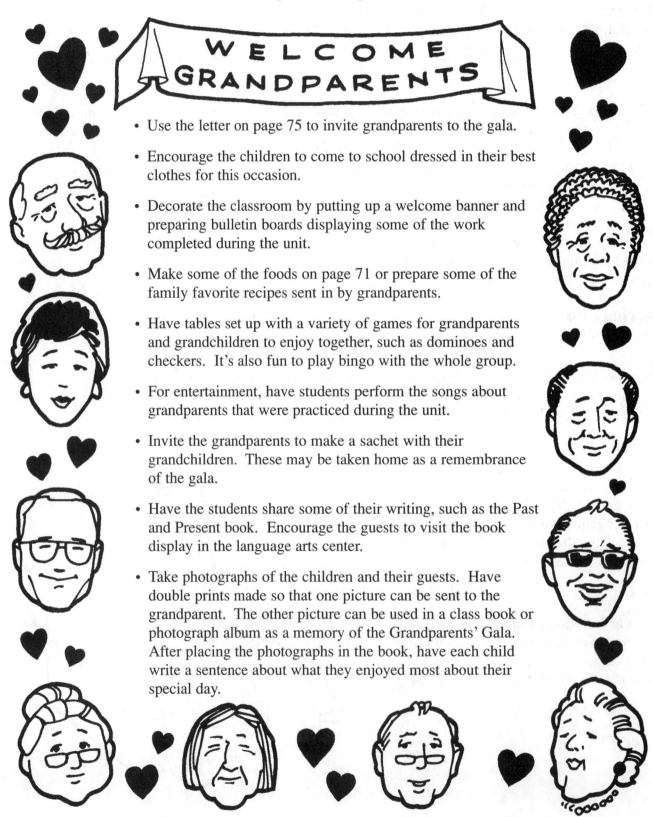

WELCOME GRANDPARENTS

- Use the letter on page 75 to invite grandparents to the gala.

- Encourage the children to come to school dressed in their best clothes for this occasion.

- Decorate the classroom by putting up a welcome banner and preparing bulletin boards displaying some of the work completed during the unit.

- Make some of the foods on page 71 or prepare some of the family favorite recipes sent in by grandparents.

- Have tables set up with a variety of games for grandparents and grandchildren to enjoy together, such as dominoes and checkers. It's also fun to play bingo with the whole group.

- For entertainment, have students perform the songs about grandparents that were practiced during the unit.

- Invite the grandparents to make a sachet with their grandchildren. These may be taken home as a remembrance of the gala.

- Have the students share some of their writing, such as the Past and Present book. Encourage the guests to visit the book display in the language arts center.

- Take photographs of the children and their guests. Have double prints made so that one picture can be sent to the grandparent. The other picture can be used in a class book or photograph album as a memory of the Grandparents' Gala. After placing the photographs in the book, have each child write a sentence about what they enjoyed most about their special day.

74

Grandparent Letter

Dear Grandparents and Parents,

We are starting a new theme unit about Grandparents. Our class will read many books about grandparents and our featured stories will be *Tanya's Reunion* by Valerie Flournoy and *Grandfather's Lovesong* by Reeve Lindbergh. We have planned many activities which will involve reading, writing, math, art, science, and social studies.

One of our activities will be to set up a grandparents' gallery of photographs. We would like to have one or two photographs of your child's grandparents to display on one of our bulletin boards. Please send the pictures by _____. They will be returned to you.

At the end of this unit, we would like to invite grandparents to a Grandparents' Gala, which will be held on _____ at _____. We will be serving refreshments, playing games such as dominoes and checkers, singing songs, sharing books written by the children, and making a sachet as a souvenir of this celebration.

If your child does not have a grandparent available for the gala, a parent, babysitter, relative, or senior friend is certainly welcome to attend.

Please send back the reservation slip below so that we can start to plan this event to honor our grandparents.

Thank you for your help and cooperation!

Sincerely,

_____

- -

Please check the box that applies and return the slip by_____.

Child's Name_____

☐ My child's grandparent (or grandparents) will be attending the gala on_____at

_____. Their names are_____.

☐ My child's grandparents are not able to attend. My child's guest or guests will be

_____

_____.

Grandparent Stationery

Choose a border from those on this page to duplicate at the top of lined or plain paper. This special stationery could be used for letters to grandparents, projects at your writing center, gala invitation, notes to send home, awards, or homework reminders.

United States Map

Use this map as needed in your unit about grandparents. Children may locate where their grandparents live, identify different regions of the United States, create their own weather maps, or plot their route for a trip with a grandparent.

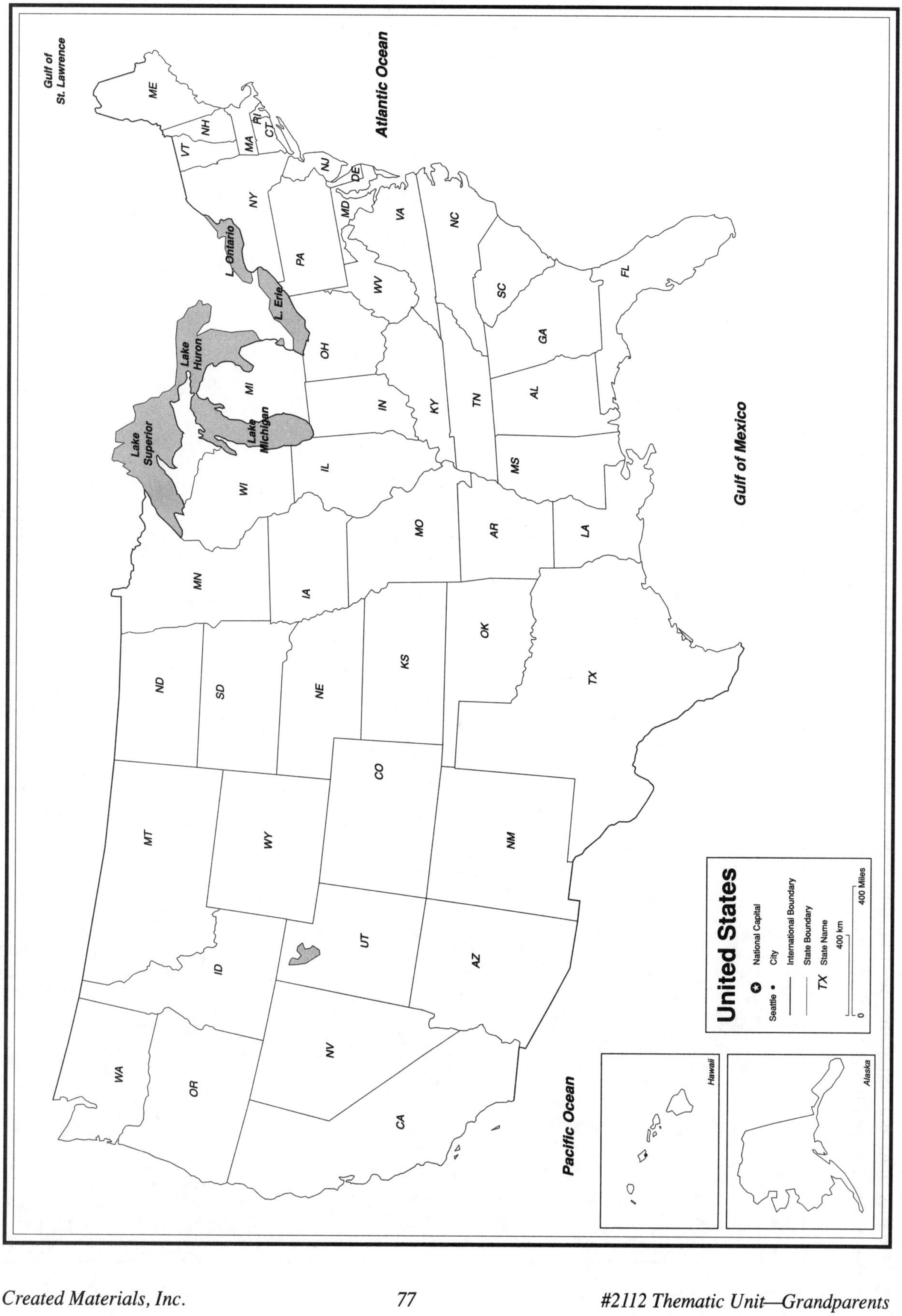

United States

- ⊛ National Capital
- Seattle • City
- ——— International Boundary
- ——— State Boundary
- *TX* State Name

400 km
400 Miles

World Map

Use this map as needed in your unit about grandparents. Children may locate where their grandparents live, from which country ancestors originally came, identify different regions, or plot their route for a trip with a grandparent.

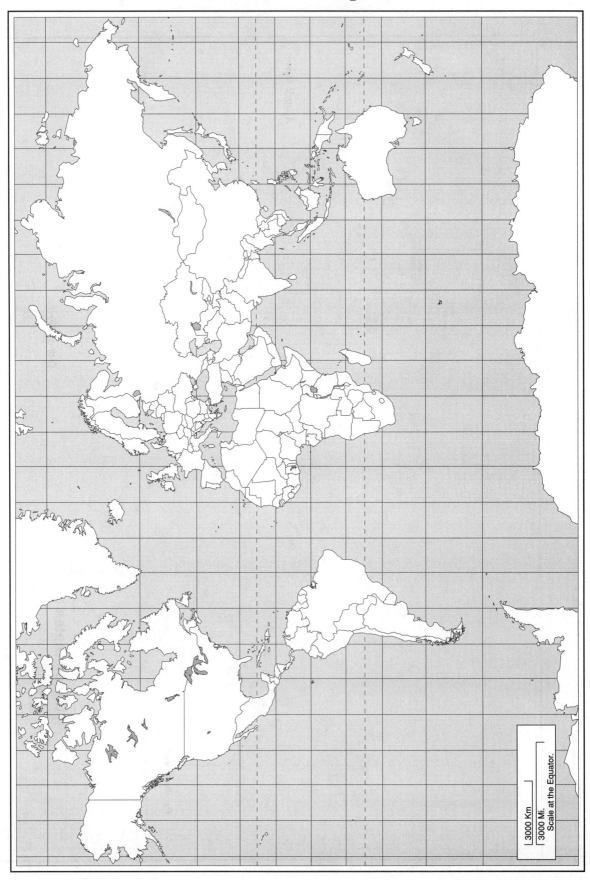

3000 Km
3000 Mi.
Scale at the Equator.

Bibliography

Selected Grandparent Literature

Ackerman, Karen. *Song and Dance Man.* Knopf, 1988.

Allen, Thomas B. *On Grandaddy's Farm.* Alfred A. Knopf, 1989.

Bahr, Mary. *The Memory Box.* Albert Whitman, 1992.

Bunting, Eve. *The Wednesday Surprise.* Clarion, 1989.

Caseley, Judith. *When Grandpa Came to Stay.* Greenwillow, 1986.

Combs, Ann. *How Old Is Old?* Price Stern, 1988.

Delton, Judy. *My Grandma's in a Nursing Home.* Albert Whitman, 1986.

dePaola, Tomie. *Nana Upstairs & Nana Downstairs.* Putnam, 1973.

dePaola, Tomie. *Now One Foot, Now the Other.* G.P. Putnam's Sons, 1981.

dePaola, Tomie. *Tom.* G.P. Putnam's Sons, 1993.

Dorros, Arthur. *Abuela.* Dutton, 1991.

Greenfield, Eloise. *Grandpa's Face.* Philomel Books, 1988.

Gutherie, Donna N. *Grandpa Doesn't Know it's Me.* Human Sciences Press, 1986.

Hamm, Diane J. *Grandma Drives a Motor Bed.* Albert Whitman, 1987.

Hennessy, B.G. *When You Were Just a Little Girl.* Viking, 1991.

Henriod, Lorraine. *Grandma's Wheelchair.* Albert Whitman, 1982.

Hoffman, Mary and Joanna Burroughes. *My Grandma Has Black Hair.* Dial Books for Young Readers, 1988.

Humphrey, Paul. *In Grandma's Day.* Steck-Vaughn, 1995.

Johnson, Angela. *Tell Me a Story, Mama.* Orchard Books, 1989.

Johnson, Angela. *When I Am Old with You.* Orchard Books, 1990.

Johnston, Tony. *Grandpa's Song.* Dial Books, 1991.

Kibbey, Marsha. *The Helping Place.* Carolrhoda, 1991.

Levinson, Riki. *I Go with My Family to Grandma's.* E.P. Dutton, 1986.

Levinson, Riki. *Watch the Stars Come Out.* E.P. Dutton, 1985.

Martin, Bill Jr. and John Archambault. *Knots on a Counting Rope.* Henry Holt and Company, 1990.

Mathis, Sharon Bell. *The Hundred Penny Box.* Viking, 1975.

Moore, Elaine. *Grandma's Garden.* Lothrop, 1994.

Munsch, Robert. *Love You Forever.* Firefly, 1986.

Nelson, Vaunda M. *Always Grandma.* Putnam, 1988.

Polacco, Patricia. *The Keeping Quilt.* Simon and Schuster Books for Young Readers, 1988.

Rylant, Cynthia. *The Relatives Came.* Macmillan, 1985.

Rylant, Cynthia. *When I Was Young in the Mountains.* Dutton, 1982.

Say, Allen. *Grandfather's Journey.* Scholastic, 1993.

Shelby, Anne. *Homeplace.* Orchard, 1995.

Simon, Norma. *All Kinds of Families.* Albert Whitman and Company, 1976.

Wallace, Ian. *Chin Chiang and the Dragon's Dance.* Atheneum, 1984.

Background Information

Bennett, David. *Rain.* Bantam, 1988.

Bennett, David. *Seasons.* Bantam, 1988.

Branley, Franklyn M. *Sunshine Makes the Seasons.* Harper & Row, 1985.

Borden, Louise. *Caps, Hats, Socks, and Mittens: A Book About the Four Seasons.* Scholastic, 1989.

Brown, Margaret Wise. *Goodnight Moon.* Harper & Row, 1947.

Cerbus, Deborah Plona and Rice, Cheryl Feichtenbiner. *Easy Theme Readers: Changing Seasons.* TCM, 1996.

dePaola, Tomie. *The Cloud Book.* Holiday House, 1975.

Derks, Scott, ed. *The Value of a Dollar: Prices and Incomes in the U.S.* Detroit: Gale Research Inc., 1994.

Dorling Kindersley. *Eye Openers: Farm Animals.* Aladdin Books, 1991.

Fowler, Allan. *How Do You Know It's Fall?* Childrens Press, 1992.

Fowler, Allan. *How Do You Know It's Spring?* Childrens Press, 1991.

Fowler, Allan. *How Do You Know It's Summer?* Childrens Press, 1992.

Fowler, Allan. *How Do You Know It's Winter?* Childrens Press, 1991.

Fowler, Allan. *What's the Weather Today?* Childrens Press, 1991.

Fowler, Allan. *When a Storm Comes Up.* Childrens Press, 1995.

Gibbons, Gail. *The Seasons of Arnold's Apple Tree.* HBJ, 1984.

Gibbons, Gail. *Weather Words and What They Mean.* Holiday House, 1990.

Jacobsen, Karen. *Farm Animals.* Childrens Press, 1981.

Jeunesse, Gallimard and Pascale de Bourgoing. *Weather.* Scholastic, 1989.

Kalman, Bobbie. *Historic Communities: Games from Long Ago.* Crabtree Publishing, 1995.

Kalman, Bobbie. *Historic Communities: A One-Room School.* Crabtree Publishing, 1994.

Krensky, Stephen. *Snow and Ice.* Scholastic, 1989.

Lindbergh, Reeve. *Benjamin's Barn.* Dial Books for Young Readers, 1990.

Lindbergh, Reeve. *The Midnight Farm.* Dial Books for Young Readers, 1987.

Locker, Thomas. *Family Farm.* Dial Books, 1988.

Locker, Thomas. *The Mare on the Hill.* Dial Books, 1985.

Provensen, Alice. *The Buck Stops Here.* Harper & Row, 1990.

Rogers, Paul. *What Will the Weather Be Like Today?* Greenwillow, 1989.

Usborne, *Farm Animals.* EDC Publishing, 1993.

Poetry

Adoff, Arnold. *In for Winter, Out for Spring.* HBJ, 1991.

Hoberman, Mary Ann. *Fathers, Mothers, Sister, Brothers: A Collection of Family Poems.* Puffin Books, 1991.

Answer Key

Page 19 (Farm Story Problems)

1. 6
2. 2
3. 10
4. 7
5. 9
6. 5

Page 29 (Read a Weather Map)

1. south
2. east (Atlantic)
3. north
4. Pacific
5. north
6. Washington, D.C.
7. Mexico
8. Answers will vary.

Page 30 (Seasonal Logic)

	Spring	Summer	Fall	Winter
Grandfather	O	X	X	X
the boy	X	X	O	X
the dog	X	X	X	O

summer

Page 31 (A Map for Your Day with Grandfather)

1. Jentown
2. north or west
3. west
4. Bert
5. east
6. Deer Woods
7. south or west

Page 45 (Grandparent Word Problems)

1. 4
2. 9
3. 5
4. 12
5. 2
6. 9

Page 48 (Past and Present Calculator Math)

1. $.70
2. $9.65
3. $7.35
4. $1.19
5. $6.16
6. $64.05

Bonus Questions:

1. $49.26
2. $132.73
3. $83.47